MAP MY PLANET

D1630827

BY HARRIET BRUNDLE

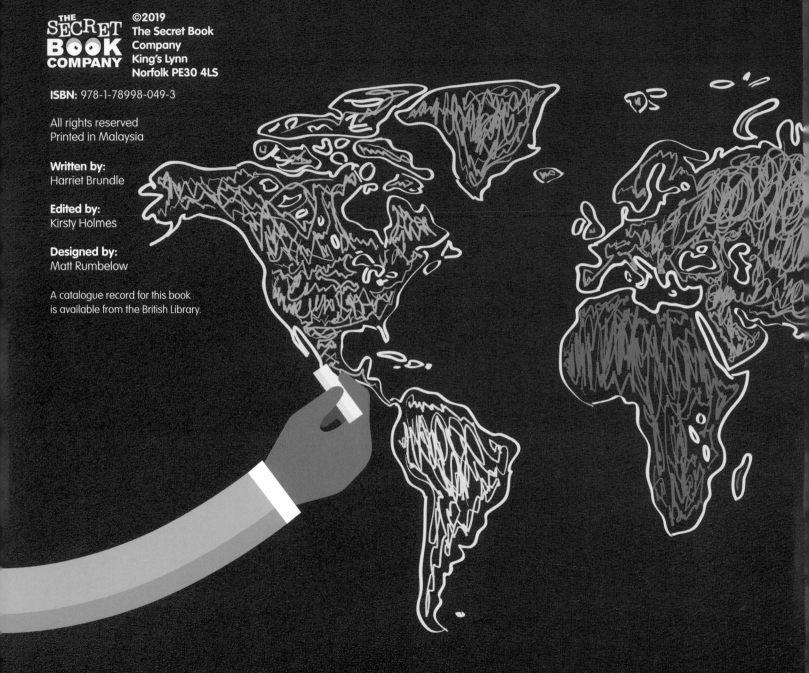

THE SECRET BOOK COMPANY

©2019
The Secret Book
Company
King's Lynn
Norfolk PE30 4LS

ISBN: 978-1-78998-049-3

Written by:
Harriet Brundle

Edited by:
Kirsty Holmes

Designed by:
Matt Rumbelow

A catalogue record for this book
is available from the British Library.

CONTENTS

Words that look like **this** can be found in the glossary on page 24.

WHAT IS A MAP?

A map is a picture that gives us information about an area. Maps can show us lots of different things, such as roads, population or weather.

Maps help us when we are in a new place.

A map could be on paper or it could be digital.
This means we look at it on a screen.

Digital
map

USING A MAP

Maps have different colours or **symbols** that **represent** places, countries and landmarks you can find.

This map key shows which colour represents each continent.

6

You can use a map key to check what the symbols or colours mean.

HOUSE

DIRECTIONS

CAFÉ

PETROL

TELEPHONE

FOOD

Most maps are drawn from a 'bird's-eye view'. This means that they show you how the area looks from above.

This is a bird's-eye view of Europe.

Each map usually has a **compass** printed on it, to show you which way on the map is north, south, east or west.

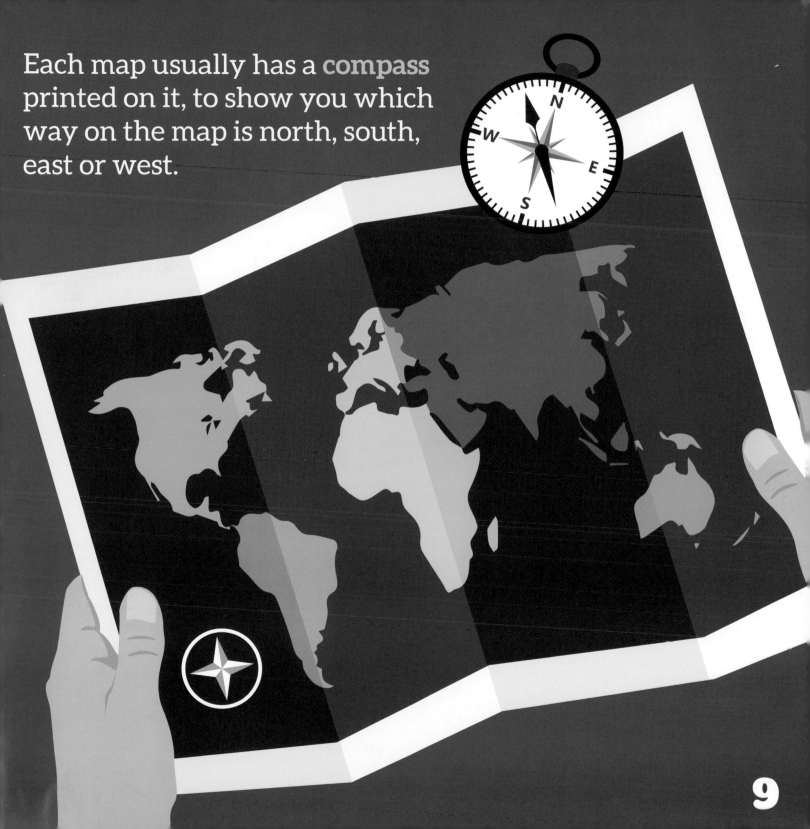

SCALE

Everything on a map
has been made smaller,
or 'scaled down' to fit.

The amount by
which something
is made smaller is
called the scale.

A scale means we can use the map to show distance. If you want to know the distance across a group of countries, you could use the map scale.

1 centimetre = 100 kilometres

WORLD MAPS

A world map is a map that shows the Earth's surface.

ATLANTIC OCEAN

PACIFIC OCEAN

It also shows us
the different oceans.

World maps show
us all the countries
in the world.

ARCTIC
OCEAN

PACIFIC
OCEAN

INDIAN
OCEAN

PATH

WHY MIGHT I USE A MAP OF THE WORLD?

You might use a map of the world to find out which continents are near to each other.

You can also find out where the seven continents are.

North America

South America

Antarctica

Europe

Africa

Asia

Australia

If you have ever been to a different country or there is somewhere you would like to go, you could use a world map to find where it is.

HOW IS A WORLD MAP MADE?

To make a map of the world, start by drawing the outlines of the larger areas of land.

There are five main oceans to be added, too.

Then add the
different countries
that make up
each continent.

MAPPING MY PLANET

PICK A STARTING POINT

Using a world map, start by drawing the country where you live and the other countries around it.

ADD OTHER COUNTRIES

Now add as many other countries as you can. You could also add labels to show which country is which.

NORWAY

SWEDEN

FINLAND

ESTONIA

LATVIA

LITHUANIA

IRELAND

UNITED KINGDOM

NETHERLANDS

BELGIUM

GERMANY

POLAND

CZECH REPUBLIC

SLOVAKIA

FRANCE

Z.

AUSTRIA

HUNGARY

MOLDOVA

ROMANIA

SLOVENIA

CROATIA

PORTUGAL

SPAIN

ITALY

BOSNIA AND HERZEGOVINA

SERBIA

BULGARIA

F.Y.R.O.M

ALB.

GREECE

ADD THE OCEANS

Add the oceans all around
the countries you have drawn.

Colour
them in to
add colour
to your map.

MAKE A KEY

Draw symbols for the countries and oceans to create a map key.

Is there anything else you think you could add to your key?

TOWN

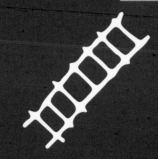

TRAIN TRACKS

FARM

CITY

LANDMARK

FOREST

OCEAN

MOUNTAINS

DESERT

ACTIVITY

This is a map of the world. The borders of some of the largest countries on Earth have been marked with dotted lines.

We've added
a few clues
to help you!

Using another map
of the world, can you
work out which country
is which on this map?

23

GLOSSARY AND INDEX

GLOSSARY

area a specific place, for example land

compass a piece of equipment that can be used to show you north, south, east or west

continent a very large area of land on Earth, made up of many countries

distance the space between two points

Europe a continent

outlines lines showing the shape of an object

population the number of things living in a particular place, for example people

represent to act on behalf of something else

surface the outer part of something

symbols marks or pictures to show an object

INDEX